Natalia's
baptism
Sunday, January 5, 2020

We love you so much,
Sweet Natalia!

Grandma +
Grandpa
Meschak

A Gift For:

_____

From:

_____

Then he said to her, "Daughter, your faith has healed you. Go in peace."

Luke 8:48

BIBLE BLESSINGS for Your BABY GIRL

50 Scriptures and Prayers

Copyright © 2015 Hallmark Licensing, LLC

Published by Hallmark Gift Books,
a division of Hallmark Cards, Inc.,
Kansas City, MO 64141
Visit us on the Web at Hallmark.com.

All rights reserved. No part of this publication may be reproduced, transmitted, or stored in any form or by any means without the prior written permission of the publisher.

Scripture taken from the HOLY BIBLE: NEW INTERNATIONAL VERSION®. NIV®. Copyright © 1973, 1978, 1984 by International Bible Society. Used by permission of Zondervan.

Editorial Director and Writer: Delia Berrigan
Art Director: Chris Opheim
Designer: Laura Elsenraat
Production Designer: Dan Horton

ISBN: 978-1-59530-801-6
BOK2240

Made in China

BIBLE BLESSINGS *for Your* BABY GIRL

50 Scriptures and Prayers

By Delia Berrigan

Hallmark

Before I formed you in the womb I knew you, before you were born I set you apart.

Jeremiah 1:5

God knew you were going to join our family before anyone else. We thank God every day for bringing you to us.

So do not fear, for I am with you;
do not be dismayed, for I am your God.
I will strengthen you and help you.

Isaiah 41:10

God is always with you.
You have nothing to fear,
because you will never be alone.

I am with you and will watch over you wherever you go, and I will bring you back to this land. I will not leave you until I have done what I have promised you.

Genesis 28:15

God has a plan for you. God will be with you always and help you live up to that plan.

Jesus said, "Let the little children come to me, and do not hinder them, for the kingdom of heaven belongs to such as these."

Matthew 19:14

God has a special love for children.
God has a special love for you.

He tends his flock like a shepherd:
He gathers the lambs in his arms
and carries them close to his heart.
Isaiah 40:11

God holds us close. God tends to your every need and carries you always.

When you lie down, you will not be afraid;
when you lie down, your sleep will be sweet…
for the Lord will be at your side.

Proverbs 3:24, 26

*God will lay you down to sleep
and protect you every night.*

For you created my inmost being;
you knit me together in my mother's womb.

Psalm 139:13

God made us from the inside out.
God knows you better than anyone else.

Keep your lives free from the love of money
and be content with what you have,
because God has said,
"Never will I leave you; never will I forsake you."
Hebrews 13:5

*God will always be with you,
so you will have everything you need.*

Your love, Lord, endures forever—
do not abandon the works of your hands.

Psalm 138:8

*God made us, loves us,
and will never abandon us.*

See that you do not despise one of these little ones. For I tell you that their angels in heaven always see the face of my Father in heaven.

Matthew 18:10

God promises angels will watch little children. Heaven has angels watching over you.

And whoever welcomes one such child
in my name welcomes me.

Matthew 18:5

God is in you.
By welcoming you into our family,
we are welcoming God into our family.

The Lord appeared to us in the past, saying:
"I have loved you with an everlasting love;
I have drawn you with unfailing kindness."

Jeremiah 31:3

God created you out of love.
God's love is everlasting.

For he will command his angels
concerning you to guard you in all your ways;
they will lift you up in their hands.

Psalm 91:11-12

God's angels will watch
over you and protect you.

Every good and perfect gift is from above,
coming down from the Father
of the heavenly lights.

James 1:17

*God made you perfectly.
You are a gift to us from God.*

The Lord is near to all who call on him,
to all who call on him in truth.

Psalm 145:18

*God will be there for you whenever you need.
All you have to do is ask.*

The Lord watches over all who love him.
Psalm 145:20

God is here for you.
Love God and you will be protected.

For it is God who works in you to will and to act in order to fulfill his good purpose.

Philippians 2:13

God has a purpose for you.
God will help you fulfill your purpose.

Children are a heritage from the Lord,
offspring a reward from him.

Psalm 127:3

God gave you to us—
a wonderful gift that we treasure.

And so we know and rely on the love God has for us. God is love. Whoever lives in love lives in God, and God in them.
1 John 4:16

God is love. Love God, love others, and you will never be alone.

Neither height nor depth, nor anything else in all creation, will be able to separate us from the love of God that is in Christ Jesus our Lord.

Romans 8:39

God loves you and nothing can keep God's love from you.

Honor your father and your mother, so that you may live long in the land the Lord your God is giving you.

Exodus 20:12

God wants you to love your parents. God loves you and they do, too.

Then you will call, and the Lord will answer; you will cry for help, and he will say: Here am I.

Isaiah 58:9

God is always listening. God will always be there for you whenever you ask for help.

May he give you the desire of your heart
and make all your plans succeed.
May we shout for joy over your victory
and lift up our banners in the name of our God.
May the Lord grant all your requests.

Psalm 20:4-5

God deserves to be thanked and
praised for everything we are given.
We thank God for you.

Remember your Creator in the days of your youth, before the days of trouble come and the years approach when you will say, "I find no pleasure in them."

Ecclesiastes 12:1

God wants you to be near and faithful now. Get to know God now, and you will know God always.

But to each one of us grace has been given as Christ apportioned it.

Ephesians 4:7

*God has given you the gift of grace.
God has blessed you.*

Cast your cares on the Lord
and he will sustain you; he will never let
the righteous be shaken.

Psalm 55:22

God will never let you down.
Give your worries to God,
and you will be taken care of.

And God is able to bless you abundantly,
so that in all things at all times, having all that
you need, you will abound in every good work.

2 Corinthians 9:8

*God will give you all that you need
so that you can give your all to others.*

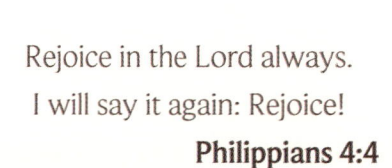

Rejoice in the Lord always.
I will say it again: Rejoice!

Philippians 4:4

God wants you to be happy.
We are happiest with God.

Now it is God who makes both us and you stand firm in Christ. He anointed us.

2 Corinthians 1:21

God makes us stronger together. We are stronger with God.

Follow God's example, therefore,
as dearly loved children.

Ephesians 5:1

God loves you. You are a child of God
and should follow God always.

Let us hold unswervingly to the hope we profess, for he who promised is faithful.

Hebrews 10:23

God has promised us hope.
God never breaks promises.

Be strong and take heart,
all you who hope in the Lord.

Psalm 31:24

*God needs you to be faithful.
Your faith will make you strong.*

"Have I not commanded you?
Be strong and courageous. Do not be afraid;
do not be discouraged, for the Lord your God
will be with you wherever you go."

Joshua 1:9

*God will always be with you.
God will keep you safe.*

For no word from God will ever fail.

Luke 1:37

God's promises for you will come true.

Cast all your anxiety on him
because he cares for you.

1 Peter 5:7

God wants you not to worry.
God will always take care of you.

Ask and it will be given to you;
seek and you will find; knock and the door
will be opened to you.

Matthew 7:7

God tells us that we will be heard.
God will provide whatever you ask.

Do not fear, for I have redeemed you;
I have summoned you by name; you are mine.
Isaiah 43:1

*God knows you, your name, and calls for you.
You belong to God.*

You are worthy, our Lord and God,
to receive glory and honor and power,
for you created all things, and by your will
they were created and have their being.

Revelation 4:11

God created the entire universe—
including you. We should thank God
for making us and the world we live in.

May the God of hope fill you with all joy
and peace as you trust in him,
so that you may overflow with hope
by the power of the Holy Spirit.
Romans 15:13

God will bring great happiness.
Trust in God, and your hope
will know no bounds.

See what great love the Father
has lavished on us, that we should be called
children of God! And that is what we are!

1 John 3:1

*God loves us so much.
We are all God's children.*

Children, obey your parents in everything, for this pleases the Lord.

Colossians 3:20

God is pleased when you listen to your parents.

If you believe, you will receive
whatever you ask for in prayer.

Matthew 21:22

God listens to your prayers. Pray to God,
believe in God, and God will answer you.

Let us not become weary in doing good,
for at the proper time we will reap a harvest
if we do not give up.

Galatians 6:9

God believes in you.
Never, ever give up doing good for God!

"For I know the plans I have for you," declares the Lord, "plans to prosper you and not to harm you, plans to give you hope and a future."

Jeremiah 29:11

God knows your future—and it is bright. Trust in God's plan for you.

But grow in the grace and knowledge
of our Lord and Savior Jesus Christ.
To him be glory both now and forever! Amen.
2 Peter 3:18

*God wants you to grow in your faith.
Continue to love and know God
all the days of your life.*

Truly I tell you, anyone who will not receive
the kingdom of God like a little child
will never enter it.

Mark 10:15

God has a place for you in Heaven.
A child's belief in God is perfect.
Continue to love God and teach us
to believe like you do.

I prayed for this child, and the Lord has granted me what I asked of him.
1 Samuel 1:27

God answered our prayers with you. May God answer your prayers as He answered ours.

You are the light of the world.
A town built on a hill cannot be hidden.
Neither do people light a lamp and put it under
a bowl. Instead they put it on its stand,
and it gives light to everyone in the house.

Matthew 5:14-15

*God made you an amazing and unique child.
Never shy away from sharing your
God-given talents with the world.*

And this is my prayer:
that your love may abound more and more
in knowledge and depth of insight.
Philippians 1:9

God wants you to learn and grow
in His love for you all the days of your life.

"The Lord bless you and keep you;
the Lord make his face shine on you
and be gracious to you;
the Lord turn his face toward you
and give you peace."

Numbers 6:24-26

God, please take care of this child, bless her,
and give her peace in Your presence
from this day forward.

If you have enjoyed this book
or it has touched your life in some way,
we would love to hear from you.

Please send your comments to:
Hallmark Book Feedback
P.O. Box 419034
Mail Drop 100
Kansas City, MO 64141

Or e-mail us at:
booknotes@hallmark.com